ART HEIST

By Jack Bradfield and Poltergeist

Illustrated by Niamh Simpson

SAMUEL FRENCH

samuelfrench.co.uk

THINKING ABOUT PERFORMING A SHOW?

There are thousands of plays and musicals available to perform from Samuel French right now, and applying for a licence is easier and more affordable than you might think

From classic plays to brand new musicals, from monologues to epic dramas, there are shows for everyone.

Plays and musicals are protected by copyright law, so if you want to perform them, the first thing you'll need is a licence. This simple process helps support the playwright by ensuring they get paid for their work and means that you'll have the documents you need to stage the show in public.

Not all our shows are available to perform all the time, so it's important to check and apply for a licence before you start rehearsals or commit to doing the show.

LEARN MORE & FIND THOUSANDS OF SHOWS

Browse our full range of plays and musicals, and find out more about how to license a show

www.samuelfrench.co.uk/perform

Talk to the friendly experts in our Licensing team for advice on choosing a show and help with licensing

plays@samuelfrench.co.uk   020 7387 9373

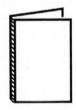

Other plays by JACK BRADFIELD AND POLTERGEIST
published and licensed by Samuel French

Lights Over Tesco Car Park

FIND PERFECT PLAYS TO PERFORM AT
www.samuelfrench.co.uk/perform

MUSIC USE NOTE

Licensees are solely responsible for obtaining formal written permission from copyright owners to use copyrighted music in the performance of this play and are strongly cautioned to do so. If no such permission is obtained by the licensee, then the licensee must use only original music that the licensee owns and controls. Licensees are solely responsible and liable for all music clearances and shall indemnify the copyright owners of the play(s) and their licensing agent, Samuel French, against any costs, expenses, losses and liabilities arising from the use of music by licensees. Please contact the appropriate music licensing authority in your territory for the rights to any incidental music.

USE OF COPYRIGHT MUSIC

A licence issued by Samuel French Ltd to perform this play does not include permission to use the incidental music specified in this copy. Where the place of performance is already licensed by the PERFORMING RIGHT SOCIETY (PRS for Music) a return of the music used must be made to the society. If the place of performance is not so licensed, then an application should be made to the PRS, 2 Pancras Square, London, N1C 4AG.

A separate and additional licence from PHONOGRAPHIC PERFORMANCE LTD (PPL), 1 Upper James Street, London W1F 9DE (www.ppluk.com) is needed whenever commercial recordings are used.

IMPORTANT BILLING AND CREDIT REQUIREMENTS

If you have obtained performance rights to this title, please refer to your licensing agreement for important billing and credit requirements.

ABOUT THE COMPANY

Poltergeist make joyful, inclusive theatre with an experimental edge. We push the boundaries of structure and form, break rules and tackle big, difficult ideas. We stage risk. We play games. Sometimes, we dance.

We are an Associate Company at The North Wall, Oxford. We are also founder members of Staging Change, a new environmental movement in the arts.

ART HEIST

Art Heist was first performed at the Edinburgh Fringe 2019.

Writer/Director Jack Bradfield
Deviser/Performers Alice Boyd, Rosa Garland, Will Spence
and Serena Yagoub
Producer Charles Pidgeon
Designer Shankho Chaudhuri
Lighting Designer Lucy Adams
Sound Designer Alice Boyd
Assistant Producer/Costume Designer Georgia Crump

Produced in association with The North Wall.
Supported by New Diorama / Underbelly Untapped Award
and Arts Council England.

A NOTE ON THE TEXT

"What you see is all there is."
– Daniel Kahneman, *Thinking, Fast And Slow* (2011)

On 20 August 1911 an Italian workman broke into the Louvre and hid in a cupboard overnight. Early the following morning, he removed the Mona Lisa from its frame and walked calmly out of the museum.

In 1911, barely anyone had heard of Leonardo's *Mona Lisa*. In fact, twenty-four hours passed before anyone noticed it was missing. When the theft was eventually reported, the painting appeared on the front page of every newspaper in Europe. Within days, this previously unremarkable portrait had become the most famous and valuable artwork on the planet.

The *Mona Lisa* became valuable because of the story we told about it. Life is chaotic and arbitrary. The universe is a mess. Yet as human beings we are hard-wired to seek pattern, story and meaning, often where none exists. Most of us, most of the time, find reasons to get up, work, love, argue, create and destroy; at a cosmic level this makes no sense at all. So, as we hurtle towards an uncertain environmental and political future, with the age-old existential questions still looming (Why am I here? What happens next?), why do we find it so easy to believe in so much?

Back in the 1980s', psychologists Daniel Kahneman and Amos Tversky proved the human brain isn't the rational machine we like to think it is. Instead of taking time to weigh up data, or consider the facts, they argued, it prefers to substitute an answer as quickly as possible. A "System One" response. Take surgery: patients are more likely to go under the knife if they're told that the survival rate is 90 per cent, rather than if they're told of a 10 per cent mortality risk. If we've successfully robbed a gallery once, we're more likely to think we'll get away with it again. Even after we've been presented with the facts, it's a struggle to substitute an instinctive belief for a reasoned one. When an idea has been framed one way, it's difficult to swap that frame out for a new one.

In 1994, at Frankfurt's Schirn Kunsthalle, a group of thieves stole two Turners on loan from the Tate. For some reason they passed over several much more valuable paintings hanging in the same room. Sandy Nairne, the then programme director at the Tate, has many theories as to why the Turners were targeted – the most likely being that they featured as the poster image for the exhibition. Once the thieves had processed this piece of visual information, it proved hard to shift.

Art Heist is a show about an art heist. Three thieves break into the same gallery on the same night. To them, nothing is more important than their own story. An audience can see, however, that they're ignoring a few major details. Indeed, that's how farce works. It's about how the brain curates the world, and how it gets it wrong. *Art Heist* is sneaking around in that territory, and asking a few extra questions: what happens when we put a frame around something? What happens when we hang it in a certain room, give it a title and label it? We make these calls so often, and so quickly, we barely see ourselves doing it. We create value without meaning to. We create meaning without meaning to. In the end, do we ever see the chaos for what it is?

Art Heist is asking if we can live in the mess. If we can see the mess for what it is. I'm writing this in the form of a play text, complete with a structure, a title and a price. I suppose we can't help but tidy up.

Jack Bradfield, 2019

BIOS

Jack Bradfield – Writer/Director
Jack is a writer and artistic director of Poltergeist. He trained on the Royal Court Writers' Group 2017, and is a resident director at the Almeida Theatre. Previous work as writer and director includes: *Lights Over Tesco Car Park* (national tour); *Garden* (The North Wall); *The White Guard* by Mikhail Bulgakov in a new version (Albion Beatnik Bookstore); and *xx (kiss kiss)* (Edinburgh Fringe).

Alice Boyd – Performer/Sound Designer/Deviser
Alice is an actor, musician and environmental campaigner based in London and Bristol. Credits include: *Lights Over Tesco Car Park* (Edinburgh Fringe); *The White Guard* (Albion Beatnik Bookstore); and *xx (kiss kiss)* (Edinburgh Fringe). Alice has also composed both live music and sound design for performance, including *Art Heist*, *Lights Over Tesco Car Park* and Poltergeist's *Garden* (The North Wall). Alice works with Poltergeist as its sustainability manager, with the aim to reduce the company's environmental impact and campaign for a greener industry. She is founder and co-director of the sustainable theatre network, Staging Change.

Rosa Garland – Performer/Deviser
Rosa is an actor and theatre-maker, based in London and represented by the Actors' Creative Team. Her previous work with Poltergeist includes: *Lights Over Tesco Car Park* (national tour); *Garden* (The North Wall); and *The White Guard* (Albion Beatnik Bookstore). Other previous acting work includes: *Edward II* (Oxford Playhouse); *Bacchae* (Edinburgh Fringe); and Sleepless Theatre's *The Master and Margarita* (Edinburgh Fringe). She has trained at Identity School of Acting and London Clown School.

Will Spence – Performer/Deviser
Will is a theatre-maker, performer, and poet from Manchester. Credits as theatre-maker and performer for Poltergeist include: *xx (kiss kiss)* (Edinburgh Fringe); *Much Ado About Nothing* (Michael Pilch Studio); *The White Guard* (Albion Beatnik Bookshop); *Lights Over Tesco Car Park* (Edinburgh Fringe); as dramaturg, *Garden* (The North Wall). Other stage work

includes: *The Tree of War* (Burnage); *The Fairy Queen* (Oxford Playhouse); *Cold / Warm* (Burton Taylor Studio). Film work includes *Pomegranate* (Requiem Pictures, short). As a poet, he has performed as part of HOME's Viva Festival 2019, as well as at Young Identity's *One Mic Stand*.

Serena Yagoub – Performer/Deviser

Serena is an actor and producer currently based in London and Paris. Her acting credits include: *xx (kiss kiss)* (Edinburgh Fringe); *Pentecost* (Oxford Playhouse), *Cold Warm* (Oxford New Writing Festival); and short film *GOLEM* (winner, Earl's Court Film Festival 2018). Serena has produced productions of *Constellations* (Keble O'Reilly) and *Orphans* (Michael Pilch) for the Experimental Theatre Club, and Quicksandance's *Ten Duets on a Theme of Proximity* (Burton Taylor), as well as producing several short films (Oxford Screenwriting Festival 2015 & 2016), and Khartoum's music video "Save Me" (released by Kodak in 2018). Production manager credits include the short film *A Battle in Waterloo* (winner, Bumble Female Film Force 2018), music videos for Universal Music (2019), commercial content for Nike, Sony Music, Renault, deGrisogono and Elie Saab, as well as extensive events film coverage including the Paris Fintech Forum 2019. Serena was recently producer on the *Off-White* and *French Deal* SS20 shows during Paris Fashion Week.

Charles Pidgeon – Producer

Charles is a producer, theatre-maker, and writer. As producer of Poltergeist, he produced the Edinburgh Fringe sell-out show, *Lights Over Tesco Car Park* (national tour) as well as *Garden* (The North Wall, 2017) and *The White Guard* (Albion Beatnik Bookstore, 2017). As a writer he has contributed to *Voiceworks*, *The Isis* and *Cherwell*.

Georgia Crump – Assistant Producer

Georgia is a freelance producer and production manager. With Poltergeist, Georgia produced *xx (kiss kiss)* (Edinburgh Fringe) and production managed *Garden* (The North Wall) and *The White Guard* (Albion Beatnik Bookstore).

Shankho Chaudhuri – Designer

Shankho is a London-based designer working in the multidisciplinary intersection between technology and performing art. Trained first as a mechanical engineer (Imperial College London), then as a designer (Royal College of Art / Imperial College London), his thesis was a speculative project exploring augmented-reality set design. His professional design work began with *White Noise* (VAULT Festival) and *Wood* (VAULT Festival). He joins Poltergeist as a set and video designer. In September 2019 he will begin as a production design assistant at the National Theatre.

Lucy Adams – Lighting Designer

Lucy is a London-based lighting designer working in devised work and new writing. She's an associate artist with ThisEgg, having designed *Goggles, Me and My Bee, UNCONDITIONAL* and *dressed* (Fringe First Award winner) for the company. She's also worked with BREACH Theatre on *It's True, It's True, It's True* (Fringe First Award winner), Barrel Organ on *Anyone's Guess How We Got Here* (Edinburgh Fringe), YESYESNONO on *[insert slogan here]* (Edinburgh Fringe), Willy Hudson on *Bottom* (Edinburgh Fringe and Soho Theatre), Haley McGee on *Ex-Boyfriend Yard Sale* (Camden People's Theatre) and Paula Varjack on *Cult of K*nzo* (UK tour). Her lighting design for new writing includes *Skin A Cat* (UK tour), *One Jewish Boy* (Old Red Lion), *A Hundred Words for Snow* (VAULT Festival and Trafalgar Studios) and *The Amber Trap* (Theatre503).

ACKNOWLEDGEMENTS

We'd like to thank Sandy Nairne, former director of the National Portrait Gallery for his sage insights, support, and encyclopaedic knowledge of art heists. Our top advice? Don't break into the National Portrait Gallery, you've got no idea who or what you're dealing with.

Robert Gibbon at Christie's, who gave us the low down on managing one of the world's most famous private galleries (but refused to give us the code to the vault).

Steven Atkinson and the team at HighTide, who have supported and mentored us for two years now, and have been such kind guides.

Aisling Galligan, Matt Keeler, Marina Dixon and the team at Underbelly, for bringing *Art Heist* to Edinburgh this year. Thanks to them the Fringe is everything it's meant to be, creating opportunities for artists from every discipline.

Sam South and the Almeida Theatre for opening up the rehearsal room and letting us experiment. Also to Sam for his expert help on *Art Heist*: The Game.

David Byrne, Helen Matravers, Caroline Simonsen, Jack Heaton, and everyone at New Diorama, without whom none of this would be possible. They spotted us early on, and gave us mentorship, support and friendship. It feels very special to be part of the NDT family.

Finally we'd like to thank The North Wall. This regional venue is doing something unbelievable for the country's theatre ecosystem. The theatre-makers who've passed through the building have had their lives changed by artistic directors John Hoggarth and Ria Parry. We are so lucky to be creative associates here, and consider ourselves their friends. The North Wall's generosity made *Art Heist* happen. John, Ria, Amy, Sherrell, Maria, thank you, we couldn't have done it without you.

CHARACTERS

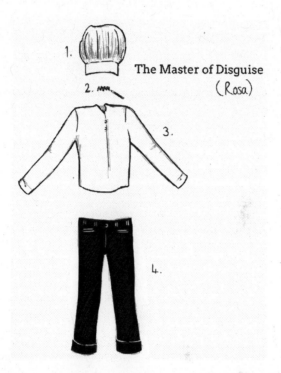

1.

The Master of Disguise
(Rosa)

2.

3.

4.

The Professional
(Serena)

1.

2.

3.

1.

The Knowledge
(Will)

3.

2.

5.

4.

1.

The Guard
(Alice)

2.

3.

***Les Choristes*, 1887**

(Stolen 31 December 2009)

An empty frame.

A few white plinths.

ALICE, *a security guard, sat behind a desk.*

There is a microphone at the desk.

Three duffel bags are at the front of the stage, labelled:
SERENA, ROSA, WILL.

The thieves enter, and stand behind their respective bags.

They are wearing white vests and boxers.

ALICE *Art Heist.*

She presses a button.

Music.

The thieves open the duffel bags and get changed frantically.

ROSA *into a catering outfit,* **SERENA** *into a stealth suit,* **WILL** *into T-shirt, shorts and cap.*

The Service Entrance, 2019

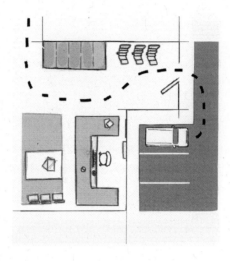

ALICE Okay Rosa, what's your name?

ROSA Rosa—

ALICE No, you have to come up with a *thief name*.

ROSA Okay. Er. Rosa Burgle.

ALICE To the point. I like it.

It's the night of the heist. Rosa Burgle is all alone.

Where do you start?

ROSA is finding the story as she speaks.

ROSA I'm outside the service entrance.

ALICE Yep. Give me more.

ROSA It's a cold night, it's raining, and I'm standing on cobblestones.

I look down and I'm dressed head to toe like a canteen chef.

Studies show it takes thirty seconds to trust a woman, but only five to trust a man.

She draws a moustache on her face with a make-up pencil.

How do I look?

ALICE It's like you're a different person!

ROSA That's right. I'm a master of disguise.

ALICE I love it. Now, backstory.

ROSA Every night I'm out taking risks:

There I am disguised as an usher getting free cinema tickets.

Then I'm dressed as a lifeguard. Free swim.

Now I'm at the self-checkout paying for a regular croissant when it's actually an almond croissant.

In that situation the croissant is disguised.

ALICE What's the motive?

ROSA You know how people fall in love with random objects?

Like the woman who dated a train station.

Or that guy who married a Nintendo DS?

That's what's happened to me and this painting.

ALICE Are you sure about that?

ROSA I was at the gallery last week at a work drinks.

And I was talking to someone important but they were...

So.

Boring.

And then I turned and saw her.

At the end of a long corridor.

The painting.

I spent the rest of the night pressed up at the Tensa barrier, just staring at her.

And I know if I just had her, I'd be happier.

All of my problems at home and at work would just disappear.

ALICE There's a metallic "cling" to your left.

It's a two pence coin.

ROSA picks it up.

ROSA Suddenly I feel a bit nervous.

Maybe I could...

Okay, heads, I go in.

Tails, I go home.

She flips it.

ALICE It rolls into a grating on the street.

ROSA Fine. I knock on the door.

ALICE It's a buzzer.

ROSA Okay, I buzz on the door—

Buzz.

ALICE And the security guard answers.

ALICE is the security guard.

Hello?

ROSA, in an appalling French accent:

ROSA *Hello. I am ze chef. I left my phone charger.*

ALICE *You know, you're not meant to be here after hours.*

ROSA *I'll... make you a sandwich?*

ALICE *Really? Okay, go right in!*

She buzzes ROSA through!

ROSA I deeply regret saying that, but I can't let it affect me now.

Adrenaline is surging through me.

I divert to my mantra.

The same words I said to myself at the Year 6 talent show,

While I performed Soulja Boy.

She goes through the motions of the dance.

I am the best. I am the best.

You've got to have confidence, or you're left with questions:

Why am I doing this?

Why am I disguised as a chef?

Why do I feel so nervous?

I don't have time for stupid questions.

This is my night, this is my heist, and I'm in the gallery.

The Rooftop, 2019

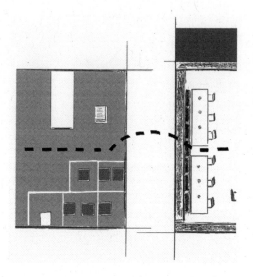

ALICE OK Serena, where do you start?

SERENA, *all nervous:*

SERENA What do I do—I don't know what to do?

ALICE Just pick something.

SERENA Err.

ALICE You're on top of a building?

SERENA I'm on top of a building.

I've got a whole Tom Cruise thing going on.

The wind's blowing in my face.

It's raining.

It's night.

And it's like.

It's like...

She breathes.

Yeah. It's like I *am* the night.

Her posture changes. Soundtrack kicks in. She's on the rooftop.

ALICE Name.

SERENA Serena Metropolis.

ALICE Occupation.

SERENA Professional art thief.

ALICE Backstory.

SERENA Total successes one hundred and thirty-seven.

Total failures zero.

An international ghost.

I move apartments every two months,

Burn my phone weekly,

I have no friends. I have no family.

I live on ready meals and Kellogg's Variety packs.

I've pulled off jobs all round the world.

Paris, New York, Hong Kong, Antarctica.

I prepare meticulously, and everything always goes according to plan.

ALICE But tonight is different.

SERENA Yes! Tonight is different because...

It's my *last heist ever*.

ALICE Woah. Why this painting?

SERENA All I know is that it's Extremely Valuable.

My client is offering enough to quit the business for good.

Meet people, start a family,

Hell, I need to mean something.

And so:

Grab the painting,

Drop it at the safe-house,

Head for the airport.

Board a plane to Malta.

Start again.

Standard building vault—

Thirty-one metres, two-hundred and seven possible foot-holes. One gargoyle.

She spins a grappling hook, and it loops round the gargoyle.

First time.

ALICE It's a sharp drop if you don't make it.

SERENA Must check the wind speed—

She tosses a coin. She times on her watch.

ALICE It lands near a chef outside the service entrance.

SERENA Ha. He won't look up. People are so self-centred.

Therefore acceleration due to gravity, therefore wind speed,

Therefore air resistance—

She jumps. Nails the landing. She's on the roof.

Standard area scan—

ALICE You're looking at the rooftop restaurant.

SERENA Glass door. Cute, but total security risk.

She smashes the door with her elbow.

Hm.

It's nice in here. The chandelier. The atmosphere.

For a second I imagine booking a table with friends.

For a birthday party maybe...

She snaps out of it.

Anyway. ANYWAY.

I breathe, I clear my head, and I'm in the gallery.

The Underground Car Park, 2019

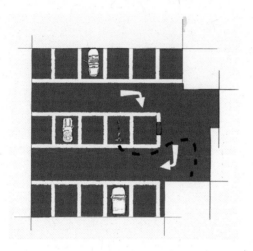

ALICE Will—your turn.

 WILL *bursts on, irritable.*

WILL Yes Alice, I *know*.

ALICE Okay, name.

WILL My name is William Hatch.

 I'm in the underground car park.

 There's a flickering fluorescent above me.

 Very atmospheric.

 I've been hiding here since sunset.

 This is what is known as a Stay Behind Robbery.

ALICE There's a door with a yellow sign on it that says Danger Electricity.

 Next to it there's a code pad.

WILL Luckily, I've been stalking the electrician for the last week on Facebook,

I've hacked his Messenger and I've memorised the code.

two two two nine.

ALICE It doesn't work.

WILL Yes. It does.

Two. Two. Two. Nine.

ALICE It doesn't, they changed it last night.

WILL Okay then I get out my hammer.

He gets out his hammer.

ALICE It's a puzzle Will—you have to investigate the cars—

He smashes the code pad.

WILL I completely destroy the system, and the door opens.

ALICE *Okay...*

WILL Now, backstory.

I've been planning this my whole life,

I'm an Art Heist Aficionado.

It started when I was thirteen,

I saw the remake *The Thomas Crown Affair* with Pierce Brosnan

All cocktails and glamour and danger.

I would spend my weekends in the library reading:

Renaissance Pirates robbing the Medicis.

Thieves disguised as policemen at the Gardner Museum.

The man who slipped into the National Gallery through the loos.

And one thing struck me,

One thing above all else.

Art heists are so easy.

It's a victimless crime.

No one gets hurt.

The thief is the hero; they leave their mark on history.

I don't even care if I get caught.

I'm even going to leave a calling card—I just haven't worked out what it is yet.

ALICE Why are you stealing this painting?!

WILL I'll tell you that later.

I head through the door.

I'm in a low corridor.

Pipes at funny angles. Gurgling. Steam.

ALICE At the end of the corridor there's a hatch.

WILL I pop it open.

ALICE It's a sewer, the smell makes you gag—

WILL I jump right in.

Plop. Sewer.

These tunnels...

Such a complex system running beneath the conscious city.

Easy to forget about it when it's dealing with unmentionables.

ALICE Something rattles through a grate and hits you in the eye.

WILL OW.

ALICE It's a coin.

WILL I pocket the coin and keep going until I'm standing under a lift hatch.

I pop it open and I'm in the basement toilets. I'm in the gallery.

Le Pigeon aux petits pois, 1911

(Stolen 10 May 2010)

The game shuts down.

ALICE Welcome to the gallery!

I'm the security guard. Night shift.

Now, this is a really important job.

And while this is an opportunity for me to see how you work,

It's also a chance for you to develop as a human being.

I'm going to need a volunteer.

Someone who is alert. Direct. And has good knees.

Not you.

Borderline.

Yes. You. Get up.

An audience member hops on stage.

What's your name?

So...er...if you could just come over here.

And if you could hold your hands out like this...

The audience member puts their arms out.

And listen to this sound?

She plays a rhythm.

Now I just want you to lift up and down to the sound.

Really good.

First exercise you learn as a guard, this.

Pause.

What do you think is going to happen?

More questions about the plot of the show. Then:

...You never know what's going to happen in the gallery.

You've got to be vigilant—

Tonight, three things out of the ordinary.

When I came to the gallery tonight, one of the taps was running.

I turned that off.

A pigeon sat outside my window and stared at me,

Like it was going to ask a question.

Tapped on the window, it flew away.

There was a buzz at the door, and I was really cautious.

But then I saw it was the chef. He'd left his phone charger.

I said can I have a sandwich? And he was like yeah, anything for you!

Then he was like oh do you want to come round for drinks on Friday?

And I said no. I've got orchestra.

I'm sure we'll rearrange.

She crosses her fingers tightly.

We're like *this*, me and the chef.

I play trumpet. In orchestra.

Anyway, look at you!

You've done really well.

Round of applause.

She turns to the thieves.

Alright.

The Gallery, 2019

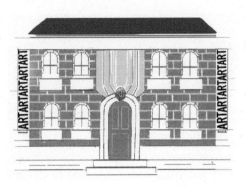

ALICE You're in the gallery!

The plinths light up, two screens taking video footage from the plinths are either side of the stage.

WILL I'm sitting on the floor of the toilets,

This is my moment.

ALICE Wait!

WILL *WHAT?*

ALICE Look down.

WILL My trousers are soaked in sewage.

I reach for the hand towels—

ALICE There aren't any hand towels.

WILL Okay then, I dry off in the Dyson Airblade.

WILL *puts his foot on a plinth, and starts drying off.*

ROSA I burst through the entrance, my heart racing—

Heading for her—

ALICE Aren't you forgetting something—?

ROSA Leftovers. Alright, I run down steps to the kitchen.

She slaps another statue off the other plinth, and takes out a loaf of bread.

It's only a sandwich,

And I am the best, after all.

SERENA I hop behind the bar, bite a lemon, spit out the pip into my hand,

I shove it into the button lock and the grating pops open.

Reach up, pull up, and I'm in the vents system.

Everything going completely to plan—

ALICE Your foot gets stuck in the grating—

SERENA Hmm. Interesting.

SERENA *tries to pull herself free.*

ALICE What's cooking Rosa?

WILL I'm finished—

ALICE It's not your turn. Rosa?

WILL My trousers are all crusty.

WILL *flips a coin.*

ROSA I've got bread and crisps but no filling, I can't just do a crisp sandwich—

ALICE Why don't you try the fridge?

ROSA The fridge!

WILL I head towards the stairs, straight through the closed stack.

WILL *and* **ROSA** *rush past each other.*

The coin travels through the air.

ROSA *catches the coin.*

WILL *doesn't know where it went,* **ROSA** *doesn't know how she got it.*

ALICE Oh Serena you're free by the way.

SERENA Thank you! Another day, another vent system.

SERENA *starts working her way through the vents.*

WILL *sees a lone crisp on the plinth, and crushes it with a stack of books on contemporary art.*

ROSA *finds sausages.*

ROSA YES! Sausages!

Fry these. Make the sandwich. Get it to the guard. Get the painting. Simple.

ROSA *starts cooking the sausages in a pan.*

SERENA I'm having trouble focusing. I imagine getting off the plane.

WILL The closed stack is... amazing, storage for the paintings not on show. Boxes on top of boxes.

SERENA The warm wind blowing off the sea—

WILL Piled under here like foundations.

ROSA It's looking perfect.

When I have her, my life's gonna be perfect too.

WILL I can't resist. I pop open a box and rifle through it.

SERENA The villa, old walls bathed in the sun—

ALICE The smell of sausages drifts through the gallery.

Everyone smells the sausages.

SERENA A beautiful man cooking sausages on the barbecue— wow it's so real.

I can't wait to get to Patagonia.

ALICE Wasn't it Malta?

SERENA Yes—sorry—Malta—

WILL *sneezes.*

ROSA What was that?!

SERENA What was that?

WILL I've sneezed on a painting.

Maybe sneezes are my calling card?

ROSA What if she's allergic to sausages?!

SERENA Come on, *focus.*

WILL /No, stupid idea.

ROSA No, stupid idea.

WILL I put the sneeze painting back and I find this old print.

It's an old illustration of the gallery.

He pulls out a print of The Royal Family Viewing the Exhibition of the Royal Academy 1789, *by Pietro Antonio Martini.*

SERENA *swaps with* WILL *and starts cutting wires on a plinth.*

SERENA Ground floor camera box.

A little bit of red wire, blue wire.

ROSA AM I STRESSED?

I can't tell, this is how I feel most of the time.

There's a lot of information coming at me at once.

WILL It's like my eyes don't know where to look in the image.

I'm here, and I'm having a kind of profound experience.

I've been preparing so long for this heist, every moment feels so special.

SERENA Blue wire?

SERENA *cuts the blue and an alarm rings.*

WILL Crap crap crap.

ROSA Aaaaaaa!

ROSA *runs.*

WILL *jumps.*

SERENA RED. RED.

She cuts the red wire.

Alarm stops.

She's out of breath.

WILL *brings out some blueprints.*

ROSA ...Did I just imagine that?

WILL I ran when the alarm sounded and I'm lost. Need to make sense of this again.

ROSA I had this flash of going to prison...

And I thought, I can't do that, absolutely can't do that.

WILL My new path takes me – oh no, not there.

ROSA 'ere is your sandwich... /NO. *Voilà your sandwich.*

SERENA It's always red wire!

ROSA Just get the sandwich to the guard.

Right, what would improve this dish?

She squirts ketchup on to the sandwich.

SERENA *swaps with* WILL, *and she studies the blueprints.*

WILL *comes to the front.*

WILL I find the door.

ALICE There's another code pad—

WILL I hit the code pad.

>And I know it's worked...

>But I hit it again.

>And again.

>And I rush down the corridor.

ROSA Is this worth it? Yes. Anything's worth it for love.

SERENA I head through the duct.

>Roll out.

>And I see the painting.

>*Long pause.*

>*Achievement.*

ALICE You're in the gift shop.

>You are looking at a print.

The Gift Shop, 2019

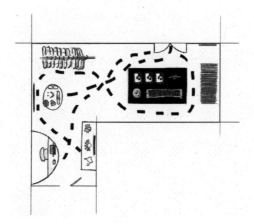

SERENA Why?

ALICE Work with it Serena!

SERENA Fine... I'm *meant to be* in the gift shop.

> Because I need to lift finger-prints from the till.
>
> Yeah. To activate the service lift.

ALICE The guard has heard the alarm, so she does the rounds.

> **ALICE** *puts on a guard hat.*
>
> **SERENA** *sits at the till and lays out her tools.*
>
> **WILL** *enters, he's disgusted:*

WILL The gift shop.

> It makes my skin crawl.
>
> Same old tat in every single one.
>
> Bouncy balls.
>
> Fridge magnets.
>
> Keyring lasers.

I know I need to head for the stairs but this anger is still rising in me.

I *hate* gift shops.

WILL *heads over to the postcards.*

ROSA *rushes on with the sandwich trolley, abandoning it near* WILL.

ROSA Oh my God I *love* gift shops.

So many things to...buy...

So relaxing...

I'm going to stay here a second to decompress.

Recapture the moment.

SERENA *has put a large technological box on the plinth.*

SERENA Just need to raise the fingerprints off the till using this lightweight fume chamber.

WILL Yes, maybe this is the perfect place to leave a calling card.

ROSA *smells a candle.*

ROSA I'm not doing anything wrong, I'm just browsing the gift shop.

SERENA I'll let that smoke. Dammit. Need some chewing gum.

She looks for the gum.

Smoke starts fuming out of the box.

WILL A little rectangle you need to buy to pretend your trip meant something.

He tears one.

Ooh. That felt good...

The smoke from the fume chamber makes ROSA *cough.*

ROSA Must be getting a cold, I am under a lot of pressure.

SERENA *has the gum.* WILL *can't see through the smoke.*

WILL My vision is foggy...the blood rushing up to my head...
It feels amazing.

SERENA Is it weird that I only ever chew gum in a professional
context?

ROSA*'s hands are covered in little plastic hands.*

ROSA Oh my God *TINY HANDS.*

SERENA *pops some gum in and begins to chew.*

WILL A famous thief has to make a statement, and this is mine.

WILL *picks up the sandwich and bites it.*

He goes over to a selection of gift-shop tat.

ROSA *has a scarf.*

ROSA What a *lovely* scarf.

WILL Not bad.

SERENA *takes the gum out and presses it on the till.*

SERENA Step three, apply the pressure...

ROSA They couldn't arrest me looking this good.
Hello police, sorry, you must let me go, I'm too fashionable
for prison.
Oh—Better pay.

She leaves a coin on the table to pay for the scarf.

SERENA *picks up the coin.*

WILL *is bouncing a bouncy ball.*

WILL I'm just surrendering to my impulses now.
It's this symphony of self!

ROSA Where's the sandwich?!

They cross. ROSA *ends up with the sandwich in her hand.*

WILL Alright, let's get out of here.

ALICE *returns, humming.*

Everyone moves.

ROSA *adjusts her hat,* WILL *hops up into the lift shaft,* SERENA *runs over to the lift controls.*

SERENA Now, just need to apply the fingerprint...

WILL I've scrambled up into the lift shaft. It's very uncomfortable.

She presses the gum onto the plinth.

ALICE *spies* ROSA, ROSA *diverts to horrible French accent.*

ALICE Hey!

ROSA *Your sandwich.*

SERENA*'s fingerprint gum doesn't work. Red light.*

ALICE *holds up the sandwich. There's a bite out of it.*

ALICE Thanks.

Hey—I know it's just us here, but you can't set off the alarm off again okay?

ROSA *What?*

ALICE The alarm. If you want to get upstairs: service lift, back of the gift shop.

ROSA *Okay thank you.*

SERENA*'s fingerprint gum doesn't work again. She adjusts it.*

ALICE Yeah...so anyway I was thinking we could—

ROSA I am very busy.

ALICE Oh! Right! Back to work...off we go.

    SERENA's *gum works! Green light!*

SERENA Yes, success!

    ROSA *and* **SERENA** *spin into the lift.*

    I spin round the corner—

ROSA I hurtle down the corridor.

SERENA /And I'm in the lift.

ROSA And I'm in the lift.

    They stare at each other.

    Lift music.

SERENA Are you...?

    ROSA *points to her chef hat.*

    Oh. Okay.

Girl in Front of Open Window, 1888

(Stolen 16 October 2012)

The game shuts down.

ALICE Alright you know the drill.

Okay can I have two volunteers please.

It can be a team. A cool duo.

This is a very important job so we can't have any jokers.

She gets two audience members up.

She asks them their names.

She positions them either side of the stage.

Stand here and here.

Now wrap your hand like this.

As if holding a torch.

And give us a good old stance.

And listen to the rhythm?

Okay and scan to the left.

Scan to the right.

Scan to the left.

You'll make a great guard.

Scan to the right. Awesome.

Do you know each other?

What did you think of this person when you first saw them?

Why? What made you think that?

You've got to be really aware of your assumptions if you want to be a guard—

Did you know the Turner was stolen in Frankfurt

Probably because it was the poster image advertising the exhibit?

Did you know, some paintings are stolen just because they're in fancy frames?

The gold ones.

Did you know that they're not even made of gold?

They're made out of lots and lots of bits of paper moulded together.

All this random information torn up and squished up and painted.

Composite. Compo for short.

The other week, I was on my shift.

I was looking at a frame.

And a huge chunk just fell off it.

I didn't touch it. Just completely on its own...

I picked it up, and there was all the gold and stuff on one side obviously.

But then I turned it over

And all over the inside was *Amazing Spider-Man* wrapping paper.

Anyway.

The Third Floor, 2019

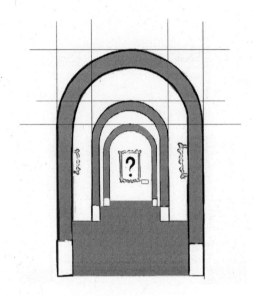

ALICE Alright, and you're in the lift.

Love this bit.

They're all still in the lift.

Ding!

SERENA *and* **ROSA** *rush out.*

Okay you actually see the painting this time!

The frame lights up!

ROSA Oh my God there she actually is.

SERENA I don't usually have a connection with these things but...

ROSA She's impossible to describe. I want to take her home and hold her all night.

SERENA I don't have the words...

ROSA It's something to do with where she's placed—

SERENA The frame.

ROSA The colour.

SERENA It's just clearly so—

ROSA Precious.

SERENA Valuable.

They both head towards it. ALICE *stops them.*

ALICE Wait right there.

　　The painting lies behind an electronically sealed door.

　　You look through the little square window,

　　And see the security system laid out before you:

　　Pressure pads pepper the foreground,

　　Drawing the eye upwards to active CCTV cameras,

　　And finally, in the centre of the composition, a bouquet of lasers.

SERENA A... hm... a little better... protected than I anticipated.

ROSA It's worth it for her...isn't it?

They both reach for the door.

SERENA But I can't just yet.

ROSA Not with this engineer person here.

SERENA Not with this chef here.

　　/I'll come back later.

ROSA I'll come back later.

SERENA I need to deactivate the door anyway.

ROSA I need to adjust my disguise anyway.

They leave.

They head over to the plinths, SERENA *works on a mainframe,* ROSA *redraws her moustache.*

WILL *climbs out of the elevator.*

WILL Oh wow.

Beautiful, isn't it?

One of the most underrated paintings of its generation.

You were wondering about motive. Well.

Let me tell you a story about the *Mona Lisa*.

ALICE Briefly, Will.

WILL Before 21st August 1911, no one had ever heard of the *Mona Lisa*.

It was just another Leonardo...

Until a thief lingered in a store cupboard till five am.

Crushed paints up against his nose,

Boots in unused frames.

At sunrise he dashed out with the painting,

Hopped on the 7.47 express train from Quai d'Orsay.

Then he was at the city's horizon.

Then he was gone.

No one realised *Mona* was missing for *two whole days*.

But once a painting has a story, you see, its value skyrockets—

And now she's one of the most famous paintings in the world.

It happens to everything!

The Rembrandt from the Gardner, in Chicago,

The little painting of a church from the Van Gogh Museum.

Why this painting?

Well, if I'm going down in history,

I might as well take a painting I love down with me.

He tries the door. It doesn't open.

ALICE There's a small electronic wall-mount to your right.

WILL *takes out his hammer.*

WILL Okey-dokey.

ALICE No, the hammer will set off the alarm.

He brings the hammer up.

WILL. You need a keycard.

WILL Well where do I *get* the keycard?!

ALICE The guard has it!

SERENA Wait who has the keycard?

ALICE The guard.

SERENA Why's this so complicated!

ROSA My moustache is so bad, I'm gonna get caught—

ALICE You've got to get the painting.

SERENA What if I can't get the painting?

ROSA What if I don't want the painting?

ALICE The guard is coming your way Will.

WILL No she's not.

ALICE Yes she is!

WILL No she's NOT!

ALICE YES she is!

WILL Alright. Where am I?!

ALICE You're in the Hall of Statues.

WILL Here goes nothing.

He bashes the light switch with his hammer.

The lights flicker out.

The Hall of Statues, 2019

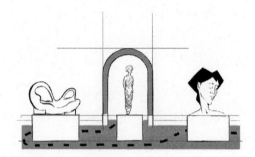

ALICE *enters the Hall of Statues.*

It is dark, but she has a torch.

This scene is a game:

The thieves are trying to grab the keycard.

Whenever the guard's torch is on a thief, they freeze.

Eventually, **WILL** *loses his patience and takes out his hammer.*

ALICE *becomes more nervous.*

She runs to the lights, and turns them on.

The thieves are gone.

There's a coin, spinning in the middle of the floor.

ALICE *picks it up.*

ALICE *turns around and:*

Lost Property, 2019

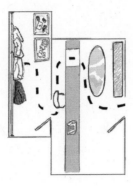

ROSA *is in the middle of the floor, panting.*

Where are the other thieves?

ALICE *jumps.*

They both scream, then stop.

ALICE Sorry you caught me off guard. Are you looking for your charger in here?

ROSA Where?!

ALICE Lost Property...

ROSA Yes, yes I am.

ALICE Aren't you French?

ROSA No. Why would you think that?

ALICE I didn't think that I just—

ROSA I think you're making assumptions about people because of their profession—

ALICE I'm not I'm... sorry.

ROSA Thank you.

WILL and SERENA *sneak around the plinths, still after the keycard.*

ALICE What's wrong?

ROSA Nothing.

Pause.

ALICE You know I come in here when I'm having a wobble.

I—ha—

I take random things out of the box and pretend they're art.

She takes WILL's *shoe off, which is sticking out behind a plinth, and puts it on top.*

The Shoe, *2019.*

It's crazy what happens to something when you title it.

Suddenly this is...

The Shoe.

Go on your turn—

ROSA *takes her hat off and puts it on a plinth.*

ROSA *The Hat?*

ALICE Hmmm...yeah... *The Hat.*

ROSA *Why?*

ALICE Why?

ROSA Why are we doing this, why am I dressed like this, why can't I draw a moustache right? Why do I feel so...

ALICE Sad?

ROSA No, like I've arbitrarily chosen a belief and a personality and then feel like I have to follow through with it with unshakable confidence, like the only thing that makes sense any more is to be this extreme version of myself, but that's

who I am now, and I'm just circling these same weird ideas
over and over trying to make them mean something—

ALICE I totally get what you mean.

ROSA Wait, you do...?

SERENA *is reaching for* ALICE's *keycard.*

ALICE Yeah! I mean I've been meeting a lot of people recently
for training.

And I talk to them all,

And you know I don't think a single one of them has ever
asked me a question about myself.

It's like—God—who even am I?

ROSA I just don't know what to do.

ALICE Do you have something you want?

ROSA Yeah. Definitely.

ALICE *gets up,* SERENA *just misses the keycard.*

ALICE That can be a problem too though can't it—

At orchestra we've always wanted the county prize.

WILL *is now creeping in for the keycard.*

Which means you're the best orchestra in the county.

And then last year we finally won it,

And suddenly you're looking at the award in the pub.

And it's just a piece of metal shaped like a bassoon.

It's like you knew exactly where the story is going and then...

ALICE *spins the keycard up into her hand, frustrating*
WILL's *reach.*

ALICE *takes out the coin.*

Okay: coin.

Currency.

Also politics.

Also opens the battery pack on my old camera when you twist it.

Also operates the slots at Blackpool.

Also a way of deciding things.

She flips the coin.

And, what's more, if you have enough of these you can buy a Picasso

And then it's something completely different.

WILL *and* **SERENA** *are sneaking up behind* **ALICE** *and* **ROSA**.

ROSA *sees them.*

All the thieves see each other,

They're communicating now.

They're heading off.

But what is it right now?

Right this second?

It's all of these things at once, and none of them, and how do you *say that*,

How do you *think that*—

I just wish everything had a little placard, telling me what it meant.

Anyway, I think about these things a lot...

I think about these things a lot when I'm by myself.

Hey, I was wondering...

I've got a keycard,

Maybe you and me could go look at some paintings together?

ALICE *turns and the thieves are gone.*

The Storm on the Sea of Galilee, 1633

(Stolen 18 March 1990)

The game shuts down.

The thieves are discussing something in the background.

ALICE *is sad now.*

ALICE Okay. I'm going to need three volunteers this time.

She gets three people up.

She teaches them three different movements.

Yeah so you do this.

One person is walking back and forth at the back.

You do this.

Another is doing star jumps.

And you do this.

A third is standing on a plinth, punching.

Don't ask why.

Cool.

Brilliant.

Not gonna...talk if that's okay.

Do you mind if I just...practise my trumpet?

She takes out her trumpet.

Begins to play.

The thieves creep up behind her.

ROSA *and* **SERENA** *grab her.*

She resists.

WILL *brings down the hammer.*

The trumpet crashes down.

Untitled, 2019

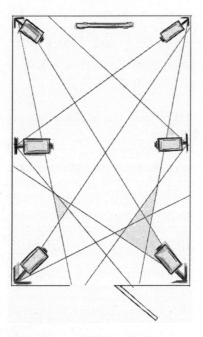

ALICE *is lying unconscious on the floor.*

ROSA Why did you do that?

Oh God oh god oh god.

SERENA Tie her up.

ROSA Is she dead?

SERENA No, she's breathing, do it.

ROSA I think I'm just gonna go—

SERENA Where are you going to go?

ROSA I don't know I'm—

Yes, you're right, tie her up—

WILL Can you...

Can you go back to your seats please...?

Thank you...thank you so much.

SERENA Make sure it's tight.

ROSA I'm sorry—I'm really sorry—

ALICE *is tied up on the ground.*

WILL *pockets her coin.*

SERENA Alright.

SERENA *grabs the keycard and steps forward.*

I've incapacitated the guard.—

WILL *You've* incapacitated the guard?

SERENA *We've* incapacitated the guard—

ROSA I feel sick.

SERENA I head to the security door and open it.

She grabs the handle and pulls.

Nothing happens.

SERENA Hm...

She rubs her hands and tries again.

I open it.

Nothing.

ROSA I open the door.

WILL Move.

I open the door...?

He pulls the handle a few times, but still nothing happens again.

SERENA *has discovered* ALICE's *booth.*

She tentatively speaks into the mic.

SERENA The door opens...?

She presses a button on the laptop and a door opening sound plays.

The game is back on.

Ha! Okay.

You're in a room...

A corridor, paintings all along the walls, floor to ceiling.

WILL *takes the mic.*

WILL It's crowded with paintings.

Loads of famous ones, fighting for space on the wall like the print I found in the closed stack. It's...

It's totally beautiful.

ROSA *takes the mic.*

ROSA And there's the first security system...which is...

Pressure pads! Yep. Pressure pads all across the floor.

Pressure pads spring up all over the floor.

They get ready to traverse them.

All three thieves begin to speak at once:

ROSA /I summon up courage within me.

I imagine taking her home.

Love conquers everything, always—

SERENA /Hm. Standard pressure system,

The trick is to only put enough weight

On the pad to check it's there—

WILL I broke into the security company last week,

Stole the plans,

Plus, I did cadets at Sixth Form—

They all look at each other.

SERENA Why do you smell so bad?

WILL It's just sewage on my trousers.

ROSA Shut up. Shut up. Let me try something.

ROSA *looks at* WILL, *and speaks into the mic.*

You hit yourself in the face?

WILL *does so.*

ROSA *is amazed at the power of the mic.*

No going back now!

The thieves set off, leaping over the pressure pads.

SERENA One last heist, then on the plane to Paris—
Patagonia—Malta—

WILL I picture my photo on the Art Theft Wikipedia!

ROSA You trip and fall.

SERENA *falls into another square.*

WILL I keep my balance, and—

WILL *takes the mic from* ROSA.

You have another crisis of confidence.

ROSA *almost starts crying.*

ROSA I know. I'm worthless. Leave me alone!!!

SERENA Give me that.

SERENA *takes the mic from* WILL.

You stumble on your shoelace—

WILL But I crash down outside the pressure pads.

ROSA *runs over to the desk and presses a button.*

ROSA OKAY, PRESSURE PADS ARE DONE. It's cameras now. Scanning the floor in front of you.

SERENA Ohhh my God.

Cameras appear.

WILL I basically *want* to get on camera!

I want my face everywhere!

I want it in the history books.

SERENA Hey, look at me.

WILL What!?

SERENA The best thieves aren't in any history books.

WILL *starts to take his clothes off to reveal the white layer underneath.*

WILL What's the point in that? If you're not in the book then you're not—

ROSA Three.

WILL Then...then what's the point in that?

ROSA Two.

WILL Then no one knows who you are, and you've hit someone with a hammer...

For no reason and...

ROSA One!

SERENA *and* ROSA *rush through the spotlights.*

WILL *heads to the back and grabs a camera from one of the plinths.*

He speaks into it.

WILL I—I cut down a side passage, and sprint past the modernists.

    ROSA *and* **SERENA** *are working through the cameras.*

ROSA This doesn't feel like a very fair contest—

SERENA What can I say? My life depends on it—you trip.

    ROSA *trips.*

    Grabs the mic.

ROSA How?

SERENA I need to leave the country—

ROSA Why? You slip.

    SERENA *slips, grabs the mic.*

WILL I might as well enjoy myself.

SERENA To start a new life! I need people—

ROSA I'm a person—

WILL I mean what's the point in any of this?

SERENA You're not the right sort of person! You're dizzy.

ROSA Woah—

WILL Some reckless spirit takes me and I can't help it...

SERENA It's what I'm *meant* to do!

    ROSA *takes the mic.*

    WILL *starts making a mess.*

WILL I start knocking a load of impressionist paintings off the wall.

ROSA You step in shot of a camera.

    SERENA *walks into a camera by accident and it goes red and beeps.*

Pause.

SERENA GIVE ME THAT.

ROSA *holds the mic out of* **SERENA**'s *reach.*

WILL I hit the camera controls with my hammer.

Cameras go out.

ROSA *is out of breath.*

SERENA *is taking off her costume now.*

SERENA You need to listen to me.

I'm on a very secret mission.

To steal the painting.

Which allows me to flee my life as an international art thief...

And retire to a foreign country—

And make friends on an island,

Oh this...

This is really quite bad isn't it?

What about you?

ROSA *is taking off her costume too.*

ROSA It's because I love the... I love the painting—

I'm in love with the painting?

SERENA That's the worst motive I've ever heard!

ROSA I could stop this right now.

Pause.

SERENA ...Do you want to though?

ROSA Um.

WILL *snatches the mic.*

WILL And NOW THERE ARE LASERS.
EVERYWHERE.

Lasers appear everywhere. ROSA *shouts in frustration.*

SERENA Can you just go away!

ROSA *takes the mic.*

ROSA Why do *YOU* want it?!

WILL Well what else am I going to do?!

SERENA I'm not seeing clearly.

ROSA What else are you going to do...

WILL I head over to the window, pop out, and slink round the
ledge.

SERENA *runs to the other camera, and positions it on
the floor.*

SERENA I pull out suction cups and climb the wall.

WILL Your suction cup squishes right into a painting of
waterlilies.

SERENA Dammit!

WILL This is a story about *ME* and I'm on the ledge.

ROSA What else am I going to do?

SERENA The wind is blowing really hard.

WILL Ooh, this is very high...

SERENA This is a story about ME and I'm dragging the waterlilies
behind me.

ROSA The lasers...

SERENA I mean what else am I going to do?!

ROSA *is frozen, staring at the lasers.*

ROSA I have a reason to be here.

I'm meant to do this.

THIS IS A STORY ABOUT *ME*.

AND I'M DANCING THROUGH THE LASERS.

She begins to dance Soulja Boy around the lasers.

Sound explodes.

Light explodes.

WILL *is on a ledge.*

SERENA *is up a wall.*

ROSA *is dancing in the lasers.*

WILL *almost falls from the window ledge.*

SERENA *loses her grip on the walls.*

ALICE *sits up, her head aching.*

The cameras are on the floor.

They all swing to the middle and pull down the painting.

They're all holding the painting.

SERENA Wait wait wait. Stop. Stop.

Pause. Everyone is out of breath.

Twist: we've all been working on the heist together.

We planned it out beforehand:

I'd get the money—

To **WILL.**

You'd take the credit—

And—I don't know—

ROSA I get to see it on weekends.

WILL No, no it doesn't work—

ROSA Yes it does! The guard can be in on it too.

And she agreed to get knocked out so it's believable.

Pause.

WILL I don't like it. It doesn't make any sense. Why would I trust you? You hit me in the face!

ROSA You made me cry – and the main thing is I don't want to go to prison.

/Isn't it better to work together and get out alive?! And go home? HOME?!

SERENA /Maybe we're after three different paintings. I've been doing this my whole life.

I'm clearly the best person to lead this. I have years of experience – what do you have?!

WILL /Well who put you in charge?! You don't even care about art. Maybe I've already stolen the painting last night. YOU'RE ALL RUINING THIS. LET ME TELL IT.

ALICE *is holding the mic.*

ALICE A coin falls out of the guard's pocket and begins to roll.

It rolls around the pressure pads, just missing them.

It's wobbling now, but it keeps going,

Past the cameras,

Past paintings lying on the floor.

It winds itself impossibly around the lasers, and then

Spins and stops, standing there, milimetres from the last laser in the room.

And then it falls. The laser glances it.

And it trips the alarm.

The alarm rings.

Then, the game shuts down.

Congregation Leaving the Reformed Church in Nuenen, 1884

(Stolen 7 December 2002)

ALICE *still has the blindfold on.*

ALICE Hey guys. Okay...how are we going to do this? Could...

The name of the first audience member that was on stage.

Could you come up?

They come up.

Would it be alright if you just untied me?

They untie her.

Phew. Thanks.

How are you?

We hope that they ask 'How are you?' back.

My head hurts.

She hunts for a frame.

I just had the weirdest...

I was in a gallery,

Like this one, but different.

This white room stretching oblong towards a point.

And every metre along the wall, there's an empty frame.

*She finds the frame, positions the audience member,
then hunts for the next two people.*

I walk down the room, but it keeps going.

After a while I stop, and choose one at random.

It's a big gilded frame, frayed at the edges, peeling,

So you can see the bits of composite underneath.

I check the note.

The Storm on the Sea of Galilee,

Stolen 18 March 1990 during the Gardner Heist.

She positions them and gives them a camera each.

It's this whole gallery of stolen art.

I hear footsteps, and turn into another big white room,

Empty frames and plinths again.

I look to my right.

She gets the other three people up.

And there's this painting sitting between two frames.

No note or anything.

Like they couldn't work out where to put it?

It's a small church sitting in the centre of a country scene.

There's a congregation leaving the church?

Or going in, unsure.

She breathes.

And the browns of the trees are sharp against the blue sky.

I look for an edge of the painting then.

I look for where it ends but I can't quite see it.

Like it's spilling out beyond its borders.

I turn and watch the congregation trudge back down the road towards the town.

I can see every single house.

I can see every game that every child is playing,

Every book every person is reading

Every meal that's cooking in every oven.

And for a second I see it how they see it.

The one book, the one oven, and then like a slingshot,

I'm pulled back, and I see it all again.

I think what a frame would do.

How it would contain this place,

How it's so much more than I can possibly say.

And I look back at the church and see how high the spire reaches up to the sky.

And the birds overhead.

And the colour.

Soon it all just dissolves into colour and I can't...

There's all this stuff.

And there's no—

There's no longer anything to—

I'm just in it.

The chaos.

The compo.

And then I was here again.

Um.

You ready?

Art Heist, 2019

ALICE *plays the rhythms for each participant.*

The audience members begin to move as rehearsed.

After a few loops, the lights kick in, the alarm kicks in, music kicks in, and the thieves begin to pull the frame between each other, and weave in and out of the obstacle course the audience have created.

The thieves are screaming at each other. They're grabbing the frame from each other.

It starts to break down. The thieves give the audience new tasks.

It's a mess.

It's overwhelming.

It goes on and on.

The painting is gone.

ALICE *comes to the front.*

She brings out a sign.

'Art Heist, 2019'.

She guards it.

Art Heist (2019)
Poltergeist (b. 2015)
Performance

ART HEIST:
THE GAME

This is a game for **2–4 players.**
It requires two **6-sided dice**, and **improvisational skills**.

One player is THE GUARD.

Other players are THE THIEVES.

In this game, THE THIEVES attempt to steal a painting from a gallery.

THE GUARD narrates a story, addressing the thieves as "you".

When THE THIEVES attempt to do something that an untrained human couldn't do, the success of their attempt is measured by rolling both dice.

MOVES

There are four actions the thieves can take:

Sneak
For completing a task unnoticed, or a task under pressure.
This could be sneaking past a guard, or frying sausages without setting off the fire alarm.
The success of this is measured by a dice roll + the player's Stealth score.

> Rolls:
> **1–6:** The Sneak fails. THE GUARD gets to make a *hard move (see THE GUARD section)*. The player marks 1 experience point.
> **7–9:** The Sneak is a mixed-success. The sneaking is achieved, but the thief draws minor attention in another way.
> **10–12:** The Sneak is a total success! The thief tells the rest of the players what happens.

Fight
For engaging in any sort of combat with other thieves, guards, or inanimate objects. This roll is +Tough.

Rolls:

1–6: The combat fails. THE GUARD gets to make a *hard move.* The player marks 1 experience point.

7–9: The combat is a mixed-success. E.g. THE GUARD is knocked out, but will wake up later, and will be on alert.

10–12: The combat is a total success!

Manipulate

For making a character in the game comply with your wishes. The thief must provide a plausible description of what they say. This roll is +Charisma.

Rolls:

1–6: The manipulation fails. THE GUARD gets to make a *hard move.*

The player marks 1 experience point.

7–9: The manipulation is a mixed-success. The character will want proof, or

10–12: The manipulation is a total success!

Tech

For any time the thief uses a piece of technology.
This can either affect their heist (**Active Tech**), or give the thief new information (**Perceptive Tech**).
The thief must justify their tech in-fiction. Want to see through walls? Do you have a piece of kit that will let you do this? This roll is +Smarts.

Rolls:

1–6: The tech breaks. The thief can't use this device again, or maybe they never knew how to use it. The player marks 1 experience point.

7–9: The tech is a mixed-success. **Active Tech:** THE GUARD introduces a complication to the attempt. **Perceptive Tech:** THE GUARD will only give the player *some* information.

10–12: The tech is a total success! **Active Tech:** The attempt is totally successful. **Perceptive Tech:** THE GUARD has to be truthful.

THE THIEVES

Each player chooses a character:

THE KNOWLEDGE

A heist nerd: knows everything about the gallery, but has very little experience on the ground.

–1 Tough, 0 Stealth, +2 Smarts, +1 Charisma

At 3 Experience Points, Tough becomes 0
At 6 Experience Points, Stealth becomes +1, Smarts become +3

Abilities:

"I stalked the electrician on Facebook" —You've done some sort of preparation for this heist. Can be used once a game to bypass a security system without rolling.

"Let me tell you a story about the *Mona Lisa*" —Your art knowledge comes in handy. Grants a +1 on any roll handling a painting.

"A calling card" —Send a misleading calling card before the heist, which puts security on guard against an imagined threat that you devise.

THE PROFESSIONAL

A confident, seasoned art thief. Perhaps too confident?

0 Tough, +2 Stealth, +1 Smarts, -1 Charisma

At 3 Experience Points, Smarts become +2
At 6 Experience Points, Stealth becomes +3, Tough becomes +1

Abilities:

"It's my last heist ever" —You're running away to an imagined location after this heist, and it fills you with determination. Can be used once per game to level up a roll from a failure to a mixed-success, or a mixed-success to a total success.

"Need to check the wind speed" —You're trained in stealth-ops. Acrobatics (such as jumping from heights or vaulting over walls) require no rolls.

"Red Wire, Blue Wire" —Lightning fast reflexes. If you fail when hacking a security system, once per game you get a second chance.

THE MASTER OF DISGUISE

A charismatic personality with an unstable motive. Likely enters the gallery in disguise.

+1 Tough, 0 Stealth, –1 Smarts, +2 Charisma

At 3 Experience Points, Tough becomes +2
At 6 Experience Points, Charisma becomes +3, Stealth becomes +1

Abilities:

"I'm a master of disguise" —You've faked it till you've made it. Once per game, add +1 to any roll in which your persona would be skilled e.g. if you're disguised as a chef, you can add +1 to a roll that involves cooking, if you're a fireman, you can add +1 to a roll that puts out a fire.

"In that situation, it is the croissant that is disguised" —You're brilliant at misdirection. Hide small objects from guards and thieves without a roll.

"Voilà, 'ere is your sandwich." —Security teams trust you. If you've done them a favour, they'll overlook the first failure of any Stealth roll.

THE GUARD

THE GUARD controls the action. They shape the story, in addressing each player in second person. They also create Non-Player Characters (NPCs), and voice those characters.

A few rules:

Soft Moves: These set up an action, e.g. "The guard is walking down the corridor towards you. What do you do?" Or "The lasers are flickering on, where do you go?" They should be your go-to moves as THE GUARD.

Hard Moves: These happen immediately, and are great for putting thieves in a tricky situation: "The alarm goes off." "The guard notices you're lying and calls the police."

Thief Moves: When the thieves make a move, it's your job to work out what they roll. E.g. if they say: "I want to duck under the camera." It's your job to say: "Okay, we're going to roll Sneak".

Thief Experience: When the thieves hit an experience mark (3 Points or 6 Points), it is your job to work out with them why they've levelled up. Have they found a new weapon, or gained some useful knowledge about the gallery?

As THE GUARD, remember to be flexible: You might have a brilliant game plotted out, but it's no fun if you're not responding to the thieves. Play to the players' strengths.

Make the game for the players: If one player is The Knowledge and mentions living at home with their mum, make them get a phone call from her at an inopportune time! If The Professional gets their kit from the black market, make sure their technology messes up every now and then. Get excited by their characters. Craft the game so each character gets some narrative payoff.

This game is improvisation based: That means you can let the thieves have a say in inventing the world. If a thief says "I run into the Hall of Statues", this is a valid move. Even if you haven't planned a hall of statues, you've got to run with it!

THE GAME

Planning Phase

Set in a safehouse of THE THIEVES' choosing. THE GUARD may narrate the action, or play a 'Mastermind' figure.
Time to answer a few questions:

- Do THE THIEVES know each other? If so, how do they know each other?
- A bit about THE THIEVES' backgrounds, as well as their names and appearances.
- What painting are they after?
- How is the gallery laid out? Plan of approach. THE GUARD can lead this section, throwing obstacles into the mix.
- THE GUARD will go around and ask each thief a few questions in private. If any thieves are planning to betray the others, THE GUARD can work this into the gameplay.
- Any prep THE THIEVES want to do, tech they want to gather.

The Heist

Set in the gallery.

- THE GUARD guides the story here.
- Rob the gallery.
- Failures are just as interesting as successes.
- **Don't play to win!** Always make choices that best fit the story you're telling.

The Ending

- The Heist ends when a thief makes it out of the gallery building.
- We're then in the end phase.
- Each thief describes what they plan to do in the following days, and each thief rolls two 6-sided-dice.
- The thief that has left the gallery with the painting gets a +3 to any roll. If they exited together, then all thieves get +3.
- Depending on the rolls, THE GUARD decides which plans work, and which fail.

Good Luck

This game is Powered by the Apocalypse System

http://apocalypse-world.com/

PROPS

Tensa-Barrier
Gilded Frame
Black Make-Up Pencil
Hammer
Clipboard
Hairdryer
Crisps
Plate
Frying Pan
Veggie Sausages
Art Books
Print of *The Royal Family Viewing the Exhibition of the Royal Academy 1789* by Pietro Antonio Martini
Wires
Wire-Cutters
Ketchup
Blueprints
Gift Shop Items
Postcards
Keycard
Empty Wooden Frame
Gorilla Mask
Pom-Poms
Boxing Gloves

SOUND / LIGHTING

Decisions on lighting and sound are completely at the discretion of the production.

VISIT THE SAMUEL FRENCH BOOKSHOP AT THE ROYAL COURT THEATRE

Browse plays and theatre books, get expert advice and enjoy a coffee

Samuel French Bookshop
Royal Court Theatre
Sloane Square
London
SW1W 8AS
020 7565 5024

Shop from thousands of titles on our website

 samuelfrench.co.uk

 samuelfrenchltd

 samuel french uk